# Fitness for Transfer

*Assessing manufacturing technologies for relocation*

J. Moss 1/01.

**Fitness for Transfer**



First published in Great Britain 1999 by the University of Cambridge Institute for Manufacturing, Mill Lane, Cambridge CB2 1RX

**ISBN 1-902546-01-6**

# Contents

# INTRODUCTION

# Introduction

## *Who is this workbook for?*

This book is for project managers in manufacturing companies who have to transfer production technologies between sites that are geographically separated.

Whether or not you have transferred manufacturing before, you will already have realised that transfers are not simple:

- Your technology might not be appropriate for a different country
- Some of your competitive advantage may come from people who are not being transferred
- The technology you are transferring may be affected by cultural differences
- The benefits of transferring may be wiped out by a poorly executed transfer that results in late market entry

Managers who are given responsibility for transferring technology often have no experience of such projects. However, a structured presentation of the wide range of variables and issues can help managers to plan better, foresee problems earlier and make quicker and more effective decisions.

This workbook provides such an approach with practical tools to assess the fitness for transfer of a manufacturing technology.

## *What does it offer?*

It will provide you with the following benefits:

- A systematic way of assessing the ease (or difficulty) of transferring a particular manufacturing process from one site to another
- A way of learning from your own experience and that of other companies
- Useful sources of further information

The Workpack at the back contains worksheets that should be filled out as you go through the fitness for transfer assessment process.

Along the way you will find

 'mini cases'

 'tips' and

 'tools'

to assist you.

## *What do we mean by 'fitness for transfer'?*

Familiar ways of assessing a manufacturing process include understanding its 'leanness', flexibility, cost characteristics, delivery performance, quality, capital intensity and labour intensity. These measures, however, are not particularly helpful when it comes to deciding how to transfer the process.

Instead, we have defined a new way of assessing a manufacturing process – *fitness for transfer* - which is just as measurable as leanness or flexibility. There are two dimensions to this new metric:

- ✣ **Transferability** which assesses how easily the manufacturing process can be 'disentangled' from the sender site and transferred
- ✣ **Appropriateness** which assesses how well the manufacturing process 'fits' with the recipient's characteristics

Together these two dimensions describe the fitness for transfer of the manufacturing process. By following the assessment process in this workbook a manager can design the transfer project systematically, choose between possible transfer scenarios and learn from transfer experience.

Before concentrating on these activities, however, we need to place them in the context of the manufacturing transfer process as a whole.

### *A ball throwing analogy is useful here*

*Consider a manufacturing process as analogous to a ball. The thrower is the sender organisation. The catcher represents the recipient organisation. Fitness for transfer characteristics of the ball can either be 'transferability' issues (e.g. aerodynamics) that are independent of the catcher or 'appropriateness' issues (e.g. size and weight) that are related to the catcher. Different balls will demonstrate different 'fitness for transfer'.*

*If you are planning to throw a ball (maybe for the first time) it would be a good idea to assess the best way to throw it and whether it is appropriate for the catcher's ability.*

# The stages of a manufacturing transfer

The overall process of transferring manufacturing activities from one site to another can be divided into seven stages, shown in Figure 1 (opposite).

In order that the activities described in this workbook can be seen in their proper context each of these seven stages is described below. It may also be helpful to refer to a companion workbook, ***Manufacturing Mobility***, which covers the entire process in more detail (see back cover for further details).

Although the diagram shows the seven stages as discrete, in practice there is often a degree of overlap between the activities within different stages.

## *1. Strategy making*

*The decisions you record on **Worksheet 1** provide an overview of your transfer strategy. As well as forming the inputs to this workbook they link it to other stages of the international manufacturing mobility process described in the companion workbook **Manufacturing Mobility.***

The first stage of the manufacturing transfer process involves looking at the strategy that is driving the need to transfer. When a firm decides to move its manufacturing capability, it must take seven key strategic decisions. These are important inputs to the assessment process described in this workbook and those already made need to be captured. **Worksheet 1**, in the Workpack at the back, is provided for this purpose. As you consider each of the strategic decision areas, record any decisions you have made on a copy of the worksheet.

### a. Mode of involvement

Is the firm going to service an overseas market by export or by setting up production facilities overseas? Although you may have already decided to transfer manufacturing, this question is worth asking, as exporting may well be an economically viable option once the costs of transferring manufacturing become fully appreciated.

### b. New facility strategy

This decision is concerned with determining the role of the new overseas manufacturing facility. There is a simple way of identifying the type of strategy intended for the facility. First, what is the motivation to transfer? This will normally be one of the following reasons:

- access to low cost factors of production
- proximity to market
- use of local technological resources

We can now identify 6 possible generic strategies for the new facility depending on whether technological activities, competencies and autonomy at the recipient will be high or low. See Figure 2.

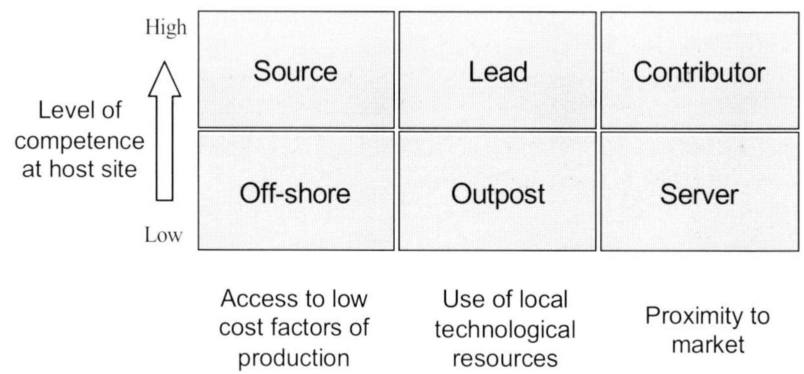


*Figure 2. Generic strategies for a new facility*

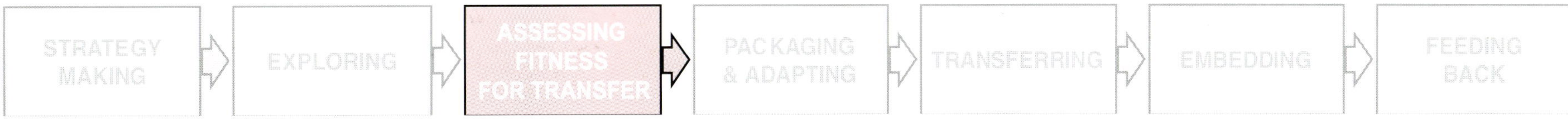


*Figure 1. The seven stages of a manufacturing transfer. This workbook concentrates on Stage 3.*

Identify which role your new facility will play. You may plan to change the facility's role over time, e.g. as competencies develop, labour costs rise or the market develops.

### c. Transfer channel

A number of alternative 'transfer channels' are available to firms. The most common are:

- wholly foreign owned enterprise (WFOE) – where the new facility will be a subsidiary of your company
- acquisition of a company to whom your technology will then be transferred
- joint venture (JV) – where the new facility will be jointly owned by two or more companies, one of which is your company
- license agreement – where the technology is transferred to a third party in which your firm has no equity stake
- sale of equipment – the simple sale of goods and/or expertise to a third party

### d. Location

Write down the country and/or region to which the transfer is to take place. If you have a number of possible locations to choose between then this workbook can aid the selection process.

### e. Partner

If the transfer is going to involve a joint venture, acquisition or license agreement, write down the name of the partner – if known. If this choice is still undecided this workbook can help identify the best partner.

### f. Process and g. Product

Which manufacturing process is going to be transferred and which product (or products) are involved?

## *2. Exploring*

The second stage of a manufacturing transfer is focused on identifying the host for the manufacturing process. The main choices are:

- a green-field development
- an existing subsidiary plant
- a different company's plant (either through a sub-contracting agreement or in partnership or through acquisition)

### *3. Assessing fitness for transfer*

Once a host has been identified the suitability of the manufacturing process and its ability to be transferred (its 'fitness for transfer') must be evaluated. Fitness for transfer involves two main considerations:

- how transferable is the process?
- how appropriate is it for the host site?

This workbook provides a structured and detailed, step by step process for tackling this stage.

### *4. Packaging and adapting*

Once the fitness for transfer has been evaluated some modifications may be necessary. These activities can be grouped into:

- packaging, which involves changing the format of some aspect of a manufacturing process (e.g. document translation)
- adapting, which involves changing the process itself (e.g. using a different technology)

### *5. Transferring*

This stage will usually represent more than just the shipment of equipment and documentation. It may also include the transfer of 'tacit' knowledge by training and the gradual phasing-in of packaged manufacturing technology (e.g. use of pilot plant and 'knock-down' production). These activities are based largely at the home site.

### *6. Embedding*

The embedding activities are those which allow the host to learn and assimilate in preparation for ongoing operations.

### *7. Feeding back*

This final stage should assess the success of the project and capture learning from the transfer in a form that allows it to be used for future projects. Typically this stage is given very limited attention. However if the company is to develop the ability to transfer production swiftly and reliably, it must learn from each of the transfers it carries out.

## So … ?

Armed with a clearer picture of what is going on in the manufacturing transfer, we can now start a systematic approach to assessing the ease (or difficulty) with which the technology can be transferred.

# KEY STAGES OF THE ASSESSMENT PROCESS

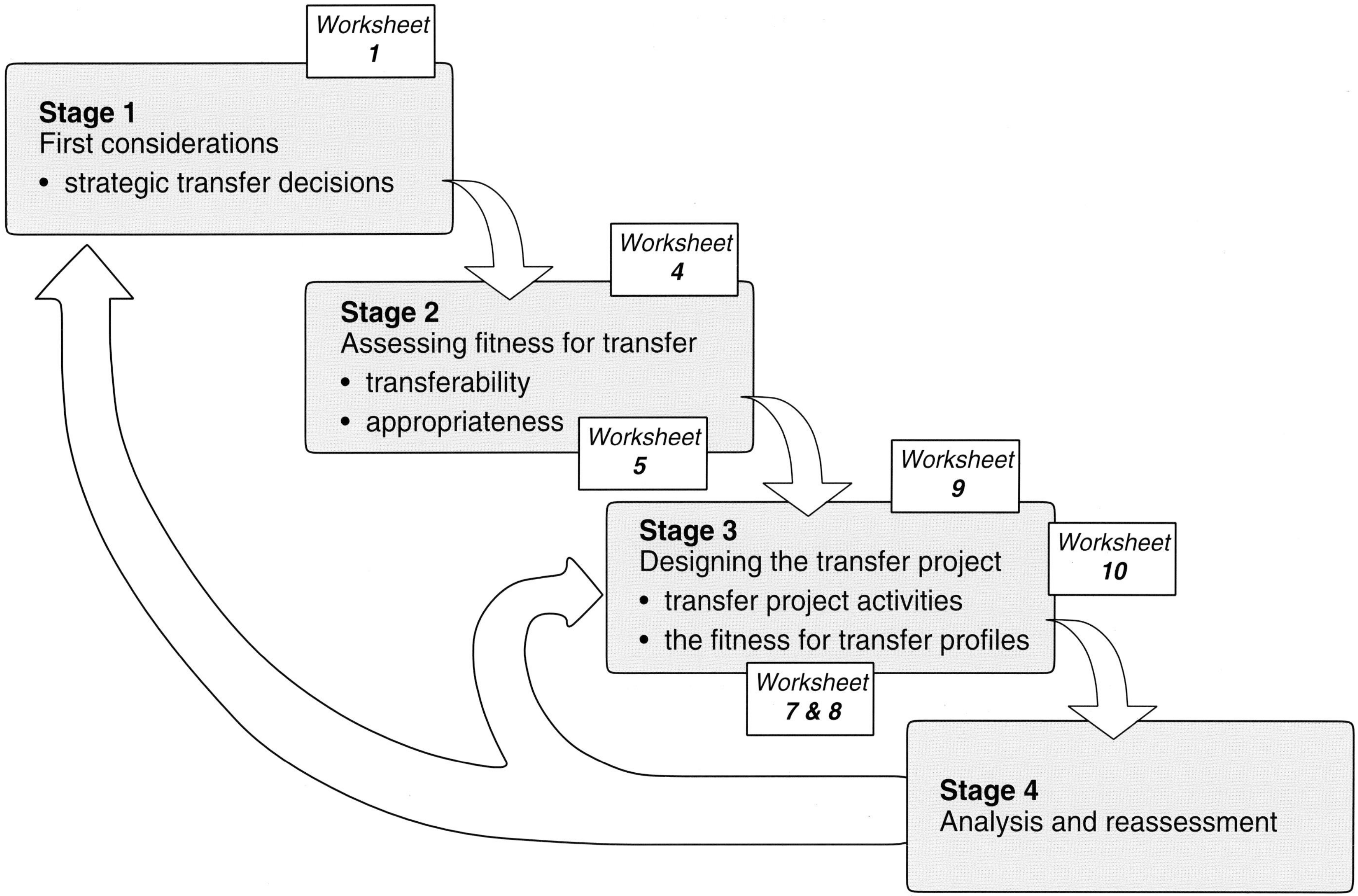

# Key stages of the assessment process

There are four main stages (see previous page).

### *Stage 1. Strategic transfer decisions*

Strategic decisions (such as location and transfer channel choices) form the foundation of the transfer project and guide subsequent implementation decisions. Outputs from this strategic stage will be used to guide the investigation.

Although you may be planning to transfer a number of different manufacturing processes, the approach should be piloted with just one – possibly one that is very important or familiar to you. The approach can then be repeated for other processes.

### *Stage 2. Assessing fitness for transfer – transferability and appropriateness*

This stage guides you through a close examination of the manufacturing process to be transferred and the characteristics of the recipient location. You will assess both transferability and appropriateness, the two dimensions which constitute the new metric: fitness for transfer.

There are comprehensive checklists to cover all the major areas that define this metric. Those completing the checklists will need to have a good understanding of the target location and the manufacturing process so this stage will usually involve experienced operational personnel and somebody in (or at least very familiar with) the recipient country. The outputs of this stage will be profiles of transferability and appropriateness and a list of transfer implementation activities.

### *Stage 3. Designing the transfer project*

Armed with appropriateness and transferability profiles and a list of transfer activities from Stage 2 you can systematically design the activities needed to transfer the manufacturing process. Ideas that have arisen in the previous stage are captured and consolidated.

### *Stage 4. Analysis and reassessment*

The value of this workbook lies not only in its systematic approach but also in the fact that it allows you to reassess earlier decisions in the light of insights that have been gained along the way.

If you want to analyse a number of different manufacturing processes or locations this stage allows you to compare the various scenarios available to you.

This final stage also gives you the opportunity to go back to the strategic transfer decisions and decide whether they are the best possible in the light of the fitness for transfer assessment of your manufacturing process.

# GETTING STARTED

# Is this approach any use to me?

The case studies used during the development of this approach showed that even large manufacturing companies lacked a systematic method for planning and executing transfers. This was because they performed them infrequently, they were managed by different people, departments or subsidiaries and they expected manufacturing transfer to be a simple and straightforward process.

Those who are not convinced that this workbook can be of some benefit should spend a few minutes on the exercise in the adjacent box. It will help identify whether there are unexpected transfer issues lurking in your firm that this workbook could help you tackle.

## *A quick check*

To perform a 'litmus test' on your business, photocopy Worksheets 2 and 3 from the Workpack and fill them in for one or more of your product groups. If you photocopy one of them onto an acetate sheet it will be easier to overlay one on the other.

You might find it interesting to get others in the organisation to do the same. This will highlight any differences in perception. For example, have someone from manufacturing fill out **Worksheet 2** 'Manufacturing process issues', while the transfer project manager fills out **Worksheet 3** 'Transfer issues'.

When the two charts are overlaid a number of observations can be made.

If any of the 'Don't know' boxes have been checked, then there is some important information still to gather.

If some of the 'Yes' and 'No' (or 'Both') checks don't overlap, then some adaptation to the process or product may be necessary.

That was just a brief test. Section 4 will lead you through a more systematic assessment.

# Other companies' experiences

Here are four 'mini cases' to illustrate the kind of problems that real companies have experienced:

A firm manufacturing cables in California transferred production to its subsidiary just across the border in Mexico. Their strategy was to take advantage of low cost labour. They found, however, that some manufacturing processes transferred easily, but with others quality and yield levels were never met. The problems arose because they had only sent drawings to Mexico – even though some of the manufacturing processes relied on undocumented shop practices that had developed in California as the process became better understood.

A firm transferring a manufacturing process to China realised – after they had installed a powder-paint line – that the energy value of the local gas was too low to run the oven. They had to tear it out and put in an electric oven. The project planner simply hadn't thought of it!

A large European company licensed the manufacture of a complex product to Korea. During the transfer, however, it became apparent that the license agreement had seriously underestimated the amount of training required. The authors of the agreement had assumed that because both companies made *similar* products it was really a matter of transferring documents and equipment. In fact, there was a great deal of 'black art' peculiar to the transferred process.

A company transferred equipment and drawings from the UK to the US. The recipient company felt that it didn't need any support as it had experience of a similar product group. However, when the US company tried to improve their yields they realised they did not have the problem-solving experience particular to that process and had to start right back at the beginning of the learning curve.

# Resource issues

The total time taken to go through this workbook will depend on a number of things of which the most important are:

- the complexity of your manufacturing process
- your familiarity with the target location
- the clarity of communication with other personnel both within your company and at the recipient facility

You should allow for about 4, two-hour sessions several days apart to complete the assessment process:

- 1 session for this introduction and Stage 1
- 2 sessions for Stage 2
- 1 session for Stages 3 & 4

Time between sessions will be needed to gather information and ask for input from other people. If a trip to the recipient site is necessary (and it is strongly recommended after Stage 2) then this will obviously increase the total lead-time of the project.

*The worksheets enable you to delegate some of the data-gathering 'legwork' to less experienced employees. It is a good opportunity for them to gain an in-depth understanding of the manufacturing process.*

Some of the worksheets can be completed by the transfer project manager alone. Other inputs may involve discussion with operational personnel and recipient facility managers as well as further time-consuming, data-gathering exercises.

An external facilitator may be useful if you think you need an independent view of your business. Should you want to look at some area in more depth a facilitator may bring greater insight or experience.

### *Project management*

Stages 2, 3 and 4 lend themselves to small 'brainstorming' type sessions.

If you have a complex manufacturing process then consider breaking it into logical sub-processes to perform the analysis in Stage 2, one sub-process at a time.

# THE APPROACH

# Stage 1. First considerations

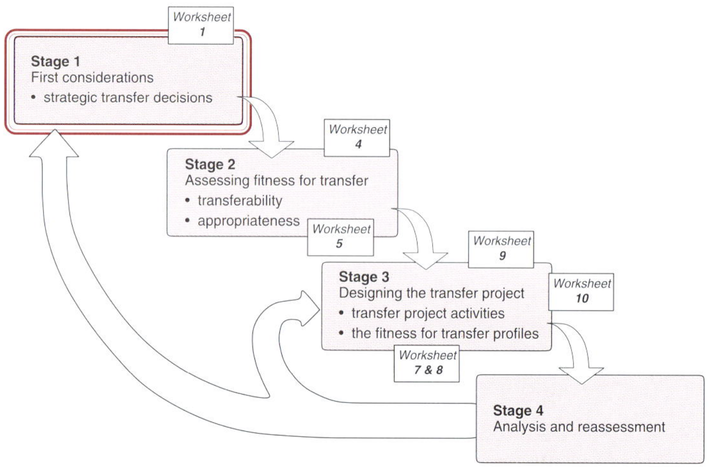


*During Stage 1 you will need to refer back to the answers you gave on Worksheet 1.*

## *Strategic transfer decisions*

The strategy at the target facility is often unclear or ambiguous. Nevertheless, it is important to be sure from the outset what the transfer is trying to achieve. (Look back at the answers you gave on Worksheet 1.) For example, when the facility pursues a low cost strategy then issues such as cost and productivity of local labour and capability of local suppliers become of primary importance. If, however, market access is the goal the suitability of the product and process for the local market will take priority.

There are a number of models that can be used for clarifying your transfer objectives. No single one is capable of dealing with all the issues. Consequently a combination of modelling and judgement is recommended. Simple models take account of factors like cost of labour and cost of capital. More complex models take account of changes in the costs of production, taxes, productivity and so on. (See references 1, 2 and 3 at the end of the workbook).

The critical decisions that you should have made in order to carry on with this approach are:

- Choice of manufacturing process to transfer
- Choice of transfer location

You can run a number of different transfer scenarios through the approach (different locations or variations of vertical integration at the new facility). Stage 4 will allow you to determine the most viable scenario.

## FAQ's

**What difference does the transfer channel make?**

Basically, a wholly foreign owned enterprise (WFOE) will allow closer communication and control than the other channels. Joint Ventures (JVs) are often established to take advantage of some complementary skills, resources of the partner or access to a closed market – and this must be factored into the analysis. License agreements are generally only suitable when the technology is well codified and can be easily transferred – because the intensity of communication between sender and receiver is low.

# Stage 2. Assessing fitness for transfer

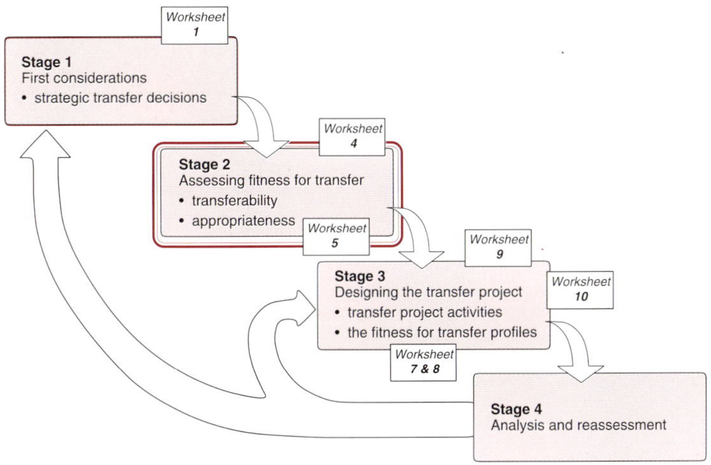


*During Stage 2 you will complete Worksheets 4, 5, 6 and 7*

The aim of this stage is to assess the transferability and appropriateness of the manufacturing process. Checklists are provided on **Worksheets 4 and 5** for assessing the most important factors affecting the transfer. Each of the factors listed on the worksheets will be explained in the following pages.

Along the way you should jot down ideas for:

- product changes
- process modifications
- support activities
- training and capability development

## *Transferability*

This is a measure of how easily your manufacturing process can be 'disentangled' from your facility and transferred.

There are four key factors that make up the transferability metric. As you consider each factor you should look at aspects of the manufacturing process that will affect its transferability. Each factor has been broken down into a number of properties. Each property should be considered separately and rated on a continuum that runs from "the manufacturing process is totally transferable" to "the manufacturing process is totally non-transferable". It is the non-transferable properties that are of particular interest because they should start you thinking about the best way of:

- packaging the process
- supporting the process
- transferring the process

For each property consider only the characteristics of the manufacturing process. Ignore factors related to the target site.

On a copy of **Worksheet 4** put a cross on the scale to show roughly how transferable the manufacturing process is for each property. If a property is not relevant mark it as 'totally transferable'.

*Extra pages are provided in the workpack for each key factor to note down ideas for improving transferability or to use as an aide-memoire where more information is needed.*

If you find that one part of the manufacturing process is transferable and another is not, consider analysing sub-processes separately. If you do this indicate on the worksheet which sub-process is being studied.

It may be useful to write down a list of 'things to find out' from shopfloor personnel. Use **Worksheet 6** for this purpose.

## FAQ's

**Surely tacit knowledge cannot by definition be measured?**

It is true that it cannot be captured. But you can see where tacit knowledge is applied in the process. So instead of relying on documentation to capture all your manufacturing capabilities you can focus your energies on training, working around or rebuilding critical tacit knowledge at the recipient site. If you can demonstrate that your process has some tacit knowledge in it then half the battle is won.

## *1. Knowledge issues*

The most difficult manufacturing competence to reproduce at another site is probably one which is embodied in your people. It is an oft-heard 'truism' that "our people are our main resource". Improvements in productivity and quality often happen as workers, engineers, technicians and supervisors gain experience. This experience is not always (or cannot be) written down.

What is needed is a way of assessing how much knowledge there is in the manufacturing process and in what form it exists. The form of knowledge will affect how easy it is to transfer.

**How much knowledge is embedded in the manufacturing process and at what stage is it? How much of it is tacit knowledge?**

The first step towards answering these questions is to distinguish between knowledge that is captured in some physical way and that which is held in peoples' heads.

- Physically embodied knowledge is captured in documents, equipment (e.g. the bearing on machine x was made easy to replace because we know it is prone to wear) and products (e.g. we have added this rubber seal because we know the product is susceptible to water corrosion).

- Personal knowledge exists in a number of different forms. It can be **explicit**, for example, "Ohm's law is V=IR" or "tighten bolt to 800Nm". It can also be **tacit**.

Understanding where tacit knowledge resides in your manufacturing process is the key to performing a transfer so it is worth spending some time on it.

Tacit knowledge is what your company knows but has not made explicit. Some good examples are knowing how to drive, having a 'knack' for something, recognising a characteristic smell or feel or the 'black art' of some activity like welding. This knowledge is often gained only after long experience of a process, is highly particular to each process and cannot be written down or learned from a text book or procedures manual.

There is always some tacit knowledge in a manufacturing process. However, it is impossible to prescribe just where it lies.

Between the extremes of explicit and tacit knowledge lies a third important category – **tacit specifiable knowledge**. This is knowledge which has accumulated over time and has not been written down or made explicit but that *could* be codified. Examples are shop practices, rules of thumb and common sense. For example a fault finder may recognise a particular test result and know from experience how to remedy the fault. This tacit specifiable knowledge can be captured in a cause-effect-remedy document.

It is also valuable to distinguish between knowing *how* something is done, and knowing *why* it is done. If you are planning to transfer an ability to adapt a process or make improvements to it, then you will need to transfer know-why to complement the know-how. Alternatively your know-why might be where your competitive advantage lies and consequently you may not want to transfer it. Table 1 gives examples of the different forms and types of knowledge.

Just as the form and type of knowledge is important so is the depth of understanding of the manufacturing process. If the effects of external influences on some output (for example, quality or performance) are not understood then any change

| Knowledge form | Knowledge type: Know-how | Knowledge type: Know-why |
|---|---|---|
| **Embodied in media, product or process** | • 'how-to' manuals<br>• documented assembly routines<br>• procedures and rules<br>• blueprints<br>• SPC charts<br>• go/no-go gauges | • cause-effect/fishbone diagrams<br>• the design of a die<br>• process control equipment<br>• tools and materials |
| **Embodied in people** | | |
| *explicit* | • recipes<br>• procedures | • theory, e.g. Ohm's law |
| *tacit specifiable* | • tricks kept in mind<br>• 'shop' practices | • rules of thumb<br>• common sense |
| *truly tacit* | • machining 'knack', e.g. adjusting feed rates<br>• controlling printing equipment<br>• pattern recognition | • 'feel' for trouble shooting a process<br>• problem solving approach and heuristics |

*Table 1. Examples of different knowledge forms and types*

*Be sure to consider the prior knowledge that personnel at your facility may have but which a recipient may not. A common mistake is to assume that what is common sense to you will also be common sense to the recipient. This is rarely the case!*

in these variables (which is virtually inevitable in a transfer to a different location) will have unpredictable effects.

Whilst completing **Worksheet 4** note down on **Worksheet 7** the critical, person-embodied knowledge in your manufacturing process. Critical knowledge often resides with experienced operators, inspectors, fault-finders, setters, technicians, supervisors, maintenance personnel and engineers.

Use a process flow diagram or layout diagram to identify knowledge at various parts of the process.

It is also possible to capture the knowledge about a process in a 'fishbone diagram', which shows those factors that affect a given outcome (see Figure 3 below). Such a diagram can be augmented by identifying the *level* of understanding about the effect of a given input variable and the importance of that variable. Suggested levels of understanding are: ignorance → awareness → measurement (but not control) → control of the mean → control of the variance (e.g. recipes) → knowing *how* the variable affects the result → knowing *why* the variable affects the result.

A French firm had developed a painting process for their product that produced excellent results in its facility in France. When it transferred the manufacturing process to Korea it had to 'rediscover' the knowledge of how climate affected the painting.

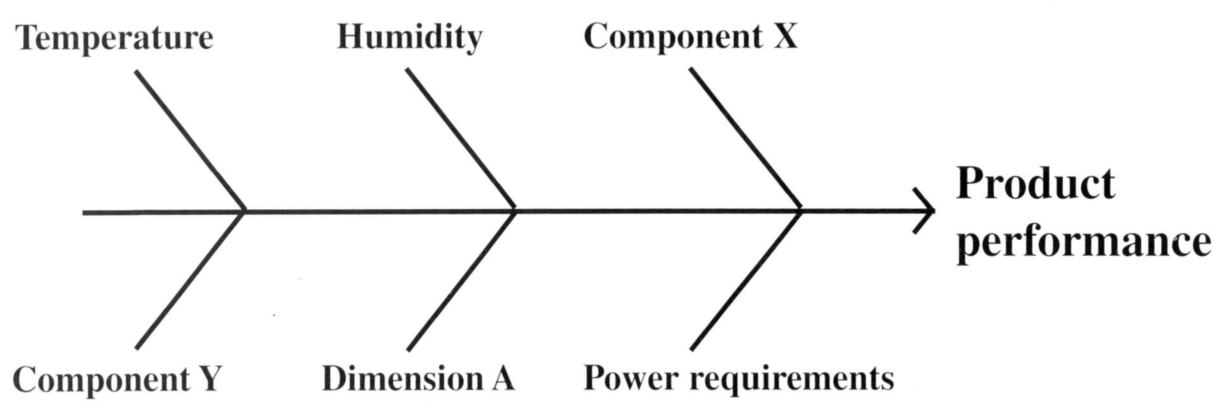


*Figure 3. Example of a Fishbone Diagram*

A UK firm transferred production from a small scale developmental facility in California to a high volume, low labour cost site in Mexico. The firm discovered that one critical piece of equipment was only delivering the desired quality level in California when operated by an experienced worker applying her tacit knowledge. The machine required constant adjustment to compensate for changes in temperature, material properties and operating time. In other words, the *operator* had a high level of understanding but it was tacitly held and probably untransferable. The process was eventually transferred back to California.

Experienced operators in a paper cup making process were able to detect the wetness and waxiness of the paper, lumpiness of the glue and thinness of the ink. These properties were undetectable to the untrained eye - and couldn't possibly be documented. They remained truly tacitly known.

Fault-finders on an electronic product assembly line learned over time to spot familiar test equipment patterns (such as oscilloscope traces) and associate them with specific types of failure. This knowledge had not been written down - but could be. When the process was transferred fault finders were encouraged to capture their knowledge to speed up the learning curve of the recipient fault finders.

**Is the knowledge teachable?**

If knowledge cannot be articulated then it is difficult to convey. However there are other characteristics of knowledge that affect its teachability beyond the tacit/explicit metric.

Can the process be tried by the trainee? Can the operation be observed? Can it be slowed down - both to observe it and practise it? Some processes cannot be slowed down (consider, for example, trying to juggle slowly).

A US firm made its manufacturing process easier to learn for its Mexican subsidiary by greatly improving its process documentation. It added colour, test and inspection information, graphical representation of the sub-assemblies and translated detailed instructions into Spanish.

**Has the process been transferred before?**

This is an important question because many of the problems of knowledge transfer will have surfaced during previous transfers. Typically:

- you will have identified the 'critical' knowledge or 'show-stoppers'
- you may be able to plot a learning curve for the process
- the process may have been redesigned to minimise its dependence on truly tacit knowledge
- tacit specifiable knowledge may have been captured in some way. You may already have a list of key documents.

A multinational company that has transferred its manufacturing process widely has studied carefully how yields rise in each of the transplants for each product type. In this way they have determined what knowledge is required at various stages (the process has also been extensively documented and video-taped), how much training is required and how long a transfer will take.

Remember to record ideas for product and process changes, training, development and support on the extra pages provided for each key factor in the Workpack. Use **Worksheet 6** to note down things you need to find out.

## *2. Customised and obsolete processes*

**Is the manufacturing process customised, redundant or obsolete?**

Transferring mature or obsolete technology can be difficult due to problems in reproducing and supporting the equipment. Customised equipment can be more difficult and expensive to reproduce than standard, off-the-shelf items and may have undergone undocumented modifications. You may need to consider adapting the process to utilise different equipment.

A US firm transferred a mature process to China, primarily to access the local market with an old product. They found, however, that their test equipment used obsolete components and its design was undocumented. The Chinese partner had to reverse engineer the circuit diagrams in order to make modifications. Eventually the company redesigned the test equipment, drawing together expertise from all of its subsidiaries to build equipment that was easy to operate and maintain.

**Is the documentation up-to-date and representative?**

Documentation may not represent operational reality. This gap between documentation and practice is often filled by tacit knowledge. In such cases the transfer of documentation will not transfer your current manufacturing practice.

It can be an exhausting process to update documentation but consider the potential costs if the recipient follows out-of-date or ambiguous instructions. It is more cost-effective to improve documentation early. Do not rely on ISO 9000 accreditation to ensure that your documentation is truly representative of practice.

## *3. Process adaptability*

**Are alternative technologies, methods and processes available?**

In the later assessment of appropriateness it is highly likely that you will identify some adaptation of the process that would improve its fit with the host site. Therefore the *adaptability* of the process needs to be considered. For example it may not be possible to find equivalent, highly labour-intensive processes or suitable humidity-resistant test equipment.

A UK firm faced with the prospect of transferring a complex manufacturing process to India found alternative technologies for its laser product-marking processes, for its networked shopfloor communication and barcoding system and for the sophisticated MRP system they used in the UK.

**Must adaptations be piloted before the transfer? Can the process be piloted?**

If adaptations are made then it may be necessary to pilot the adapted process prior to transfer either on a smaller scale or at full-size. This poses questions of availability of physical space and time and the ability of the process to be piloted.

A firm manufacturing picture tubes realised that any adaptations would be too expensive to pilot. They decided to 'clone' their manufacturing process as much as possible so that any adaptations could be piloted on an existing line at another subsidiary.

## FAQ's

**Does having ISO 9000 accreditation mean the process is more transferable?**

Not necessarily. It is a guarantee that you have a certain level of documentation and control. But ISO 9000 was not designed to see whether that documentation captures the essence of your manufacturing capability. It would be unwise to assume that ISO accreditation bestows comprehensive, teachable and up-to-date documentation.

## *4. Packaging for transfer*

**Can the process be transferred piecemeal?**

In order to reduce early exposure or in response to poor local suppliers it is common to use 'knocked down' (KD) modes of transfer. The product is either partly manufactured, 'semi-knocked down' (SKD), at the sender site and sent out in kit form, or it is sent out as a 'completely knocked down' kit of parts (CKD). This entails process changes at the sender site and the infrastructure to ship multiple, small parts (your facility may only be accustomed to shipping single, finished items).

A UK firm supplied its Indian subsidiary with kits of parts as local suppliers were not very sophisticated. However the kits were poached from the home site when local shortages occurred causing regular shortfalls and severely disrupting scheduling.

**Can the process be split into sub-processes?**

If you are planning to split the manufacturing process and transfer sub-processes then these need to be disaggregated without "trailing roots". You may want to reduce the vertical integration of the transferred facility or keep sub-processes that are difficult to transfer at home or even avoid transferring a sub-process altogether that would be operating well below its economy of scale if it were transferred.

**Can packaging the process protect its intellectual property content?**

Although a manufacturing transfer is used to transfer manufacturing capability it is often desirable to keep the key intellectual property associated with the technology 'at home'. If the main focus for product adaptation or quality levels lies in physical equipment or software it may be relatively straightforward to keep these under your control. If, however, these reside in key documents or in the interaction between two stages of the process then it may be desirable to divide the process and only transfer part of it.

A US industrial equipment firm considered its key knowledge to reside in the manufacture of a complex machined part. When they established a JV in China they transferred simple manufacturing processes and the assembly process. The complex machining capability remained at the home site.

*Assembly processes are most amenable to knocked-down production. Any process with strong linkages back to earlier sub-processes will be difficult to transfer by SKD or CKD. Sub-assemblies that are physically fragile or susceptible to the elements should not be transferred as kits.*

*The sender site may need to establish new material handling procedures for KD-type production.*

*Extra pages are provided in the Workpack for each key factor to note down ideas for improving appropriateness or as an aide-memoire when more information is needed.*

*If you find that one part of the manufacturing process is appropriate and another is not, then consider analysing sub-processes separately – making clear on the worksheet which sub-process is being studied.*

## Appropriateness

This is a measure of how well your manufacturing process fits with the characteristics of the target location. There are nine key factors that must be considered to assess the appropriateness of the technology for the proposed host site. Where higher resolution is needed the factor can be broken down into a number of properties. **Each property should be considered.**

On **Worksheet 5** put a cross on the scale to show roughly how appropriate the manufacturing process is for each property. If that property is not relevant, then put the cross on 'totally appropriate'. It may be useful to write down a list of 'things to find out' about the recipient site. Use **Worksheet 6** for this purpose.

For each property refer back to the characteristics of the target location or partner. If you are not able to complete any part of the worksheet with ease note it down as something to investigate further. Even seemingly innocent issues can, in practice, cause major problems for a transfer (remember the powder coating oven example). Some of the questions group a number of issues together. There are two reasons for this:

- it stops the exercise becoming long-winded
- it ensures that each property is of approximately equal importance

It is the inappropriate properties that are of particular interest because they should start you thinking about ways of adapting the process or areas that need to be developed.

The remainder of this section considers each appropriateness factor in turn as well as the various properties that comprise the factor.

## *1. Host labour*

**Is the manufacturing process appropriate for the productivity and cost of host country direct and indirect labour?**

For example if your strategy involves access to low cost labour are you transferring a labour intensive manufacturing process to a low cost labour area? If your manufacturing process is not labour intensive and access to low cost labour is not a strategic objective then you should mark this as 'totally appropriate'.

**Are the skills required by the process available from the local labour pool?**

Skill levels will affect the kind of processes and technologies that can be transferred. Consider what you will need in terms of operators, maintenance personnel, engineers and management staff.

**Is the manufacturing process appropriate for host labour educational levels and language characteristics?**

Local education levels will affect the viability of techniques such as teamworking, kaizen and problem solving. In many countries management and shopfloor speak a different language.

**Is the manufacturing process going to be adversely affected by high levels of labour turnover?**

Developing countries suffer from high labour turnover – a result of 'poaching' by other companies, different work ethics, etc. If your process relies on highly trained personnel this may be a problem.

A firm with a subsidiary in Mexico adapted its production layout to include more process steps with shorter cycle times. It was able to increase volumes, reduce training requirements and simplify production equipment. It also set up a short training program, built up staff pride in the company and established new personnel procedures to minimise the high labour turnover endemic in the region.

Consider adapting the process to increase or reduce the labour content or skill level, translating documents and providing technical support.

## *2. Target market*

**Does the process capacity and flexibility match the target market demand characteristics?**

The manufacturing process may need to be adapted to serve a larger or smaller market - or even different lot sizes - depending on process scale economies and minimum efficient scale. The target market may also demand product, volume and delivery flexibility from the manufacturing process - which may differ from that designed into the process at your current facility. Consider adapting your process to improve the fit.

A UK canning company set up a facility in China to provide drinks containers for the local market. They had to adapt their manufacturing technology to provide empty cans in much smaller batches - changing the cost justification of much of the capital equipment and allowing greater labour intensity on loading operations. They also changed the extent of vertical integration of the plant since making the can ring-pulls proved uneconomical.

*Data on labour costs and productivity can be found in Productivity Yearbooks or by enquiry at the recipient site. It is important to consider productivity differences which can soon eradicate savings from lower labour costs. Lower productivity can also alter the justification and layout of production lines and cells as well as shift established bottlenecks.*

*In many countries low labour costs may often be difficult to achieve. Lower productivity, special employment taxes and strict labour laws can often be used by Governments to minimise 'exploitation' by foreign companies. Furthermore increasing the labour content of your process can become a human resource headache - trained labour does not stay cheap and has a habit of not staying at all!*

*If you have a cost model of your manufacturing process it may be worth trying different labour costs and varying labour productivity to see the effect on layout decisions and process cycle times.*

**Does the product match the target market needs?**
Market access may be the sole motivation for transfer in which case it is vital that the product to be manufactured is appropriate for the local market. Consider the strategies of your potential competitors. Are they offering a similar product? Are they pursuing different strategies to your current competitors? Are they likely to stage a counter-attack in your home market? If the facility is to be used to supply export markets then the cost of shipping products to market must be taken into consideration - especially for large or fragile goods.

Good market research can be invaluable before making a commitment to set up a manufacturing facility. Adapt your product in the light of market research.

A firm selling personal telecommunication products in India decided to manufacture locally to avoid high import duties. They realised they had to adapt their product to tolerate the high humidity in the region. However, they had underestimated competition from rival technologies being introduced into the nascent Indian market.

## *3. Suppliers*

**Are the requirements for the materials to be used in the manufacturing process in terms of quality, cost, delivery, flexibility and service appropriate for local or international suppliers?**
The material content of the manufactured cost is typically large. Therefore the ability to source raw materials and components locally (referred to as 'localisation') can swing the long-term economic viability of the transfer. Indeed the main justification for the transfer may be local access to a low cost raw material. Your manufacturing process will have come to depend on certain characteristics of local suppliers. These are typically the cost, quality, delivery reliability, lead time, standards and proximity of suppliers. Consider the effects on your process of having to ship many of the components or the impact of variable quality, locally-supplied raw materials.

*List the components and suppliers that make up 80% of the cost of the product – this will normally be about 20% of the Bill of Materials. Also make a note of critical, hard-to-source or long leadtime items.*

In many locations where the industrial infrastructure is underdeveloped you may have great difficulty sourcing even simple components, consumables and replacement parts. 'For want of a nail the war was lost' takes on real meaning when manufacturing in some parts of China.

A firm from the USA established a facility in Beijing to manufacture large welded assemblies. An important concern for them was the availability of steel of a suitable quality. Not only did they have to purchase steel from the state-run Ministry of Metals, but exact or optimum sizes couldn't be specified and, due to variable quality, they had to cut off and test 'coupons' from every batch of steel - resulting in wastage and delays.

Just In Time (JIT) production requires consistent quality parts from local suppliers whose output can be shipped directly to the production line. This capability may take a long time to develop in a new facility, so consider the implications of larger quantities of goods in inventory and higher levels of handling and inspection.

Options available include shipping kits of parts or products partly disassembled - referred to as Completely Knocked Down (CKD) and Semi-Knocked Down (SKD) respectively. Alternatively you could persuade your current suppliers to deliver to the overseas facility or develop new, local suppliers. Where less capable suppliers are being used the manufacturing process can be adapted to accept wider tolerance deviations and more inspection can be added.

## *4. Host infrastructure*

**Is the manufacturing process appropriate for local utility supplies in terms of quality, cost and availability?**
Manufacturing processes obviously depend on infrastructure utilities such as electricity, gas, water and sewage. These necessities may be unavailable or of different cost, quality, quantity and dependability at the host location.

The legendary unreliability of the electricity supply in Calcutta led one firm to adapt its manufacturing process to remove the networked computer system which was continually in danger of crashing. Instead stand-alone stations were developed which could restart very quickly after a power disruption.

Until recently, firms on the outskirts of Shanghai were informed at the beginning of the week about the days on which they could expect to have power. Usually they would have one day a week without power.

Some firms install emergency power supplies to kick in when power fails. You will have a limited ability to change infrastructure. The easier option is to understand how your manufacturing process can be affected and plan accordingly.

**Are the supply and delivery requirements of the manufacturing process appropriate for telecommunications, road, rail, shipping and air-freight infrastructure?**
Consider the availability, quality, capacity and dependability of physical infrastructure for receiving supplies and shipping finished products. Many underdeveloped areas have trucks that lack proper suspension and roads of very poor quality. Such conditions can wreak havoc on anything but the most robust and well-packaged product.

Poor local infrastructure meant that a JV in China had fewer geographically dispersed customers than a plant of traditional scale would normally serve. The plant was adapted to be smaller than the normal, minimum efficient size.

While it may be outside your budget to resurface all of the major roads in downtown Tijuana, you can ensure that you have extra-strong packaging, access to good trucks and a reliable logistics company. Some firms install satellite link-ups in areas where telecommunications are vital and the local landline providers are not able to deliver reliable services.

**Is the process appropriate for the space and format of available buildings?**
If you are planning to move into existing buildings you may find that the layout of your plant will not fit without some modification. This is particularly likely to be the case when moving into the premises of a JV partner or into a country which has a different building culture. For example many of the industrial units in Chinese cities are multi-storeyed on small lots and this can cause problems for material flows around the factory.

## *5. Host organisation resources and capabilities*

If you are planning to enter a JV or license agreement then it is important to understand your partner's characteristics and capabilities. This would ordinarily form part of the pre-transfer strategic assessment. It is also important to identify any weaknesses that the partner may have.

Much the same is true if the host is a potential acquisition target. Even when the transfer is to be set up as a wholly foreign-owned enterprise (WFOE) it may still be an existing

*Visit the target site early on in the transfer planning stage. Drive to suppliers from the factory site, and try out phone and fax links. Even if a local manager says the infrastructure is good remember it's all relative. He may be quite happy to accept a 2-year wait for a phone in his house!*

subsidiary. Alternatively you may decide to establish a green-field site.

Whatever the case, particular resources and capabilities must be present at the new facility.

**Do the technical requirements of the manufacturing process match the recipient's technical resources?**
Firstly, does the recipient have the physical infrastructure in place? This may include considerations such as gantry crane capacity, machining and fabrication equipment capacity or air-conditioned facilities. It is impractical to attempt a comprehensive list here. Each case should be assessed in its own context.

The recipient may also be using some of his existing workforce in which case skill levels and quality need to be assessed. For example do they have welders, machinists, setters, technicians and maintenance personnel? Any mismatch should flag up an opportunity for training or recruitment.

A European firm transferring train manufacturing to South Korea chose a licensee who already manufactured rolling stock. The Korean facility already had the necessary physical infrastructure such as turntables, tracking, gantry cranes and sheds.

**Are the manufacturing management methods that support the process familiar to the recipient?**
Management theorists are fond of talking about corporate and company culture. This can be difficult to see from within a firm and even more difficult to measure. Nevertheless 'ways of doing things' that are unique to a particular company do develop and can lead to manufacturing processes coming unstuck when they are transferred to a different company. One of the most overt effects of company culture is the variation in the extent to which modern manufacturing management methods have been adopted. For example your firm may have a total quality ethic which guides the way you do things or use JIT, total preventative maintenance (TPM) or Statistical Process Control (SPC). These methods often take years to embed and a lack of familiarity with them may inhibit the fit with the host organisation.

If a mismatch is found then the recipient will need to be trained in the relevant methods. Frequently existing documentation can be improved to give more guidance during this learning phase.

**Do the manufacturing process characteristics match the recipient's support capabilities?**
This involves checking the elements of the recipient's manufacturing *system* that support the manufacturing *process*. This would include functions such as engineering, maintenance, forecasting, purchasing, document control, aggregate and daily planning and control and quality assurance. Training requirements and responsibilities can be identified by systematically auditing the capabilities of the recipient in these support functions.

**Is the manufacturing process appropriate for the recipient's organisational structure?**
Organisational structures vary between firms. It is generally accepted that an organisation should be designed to suit its task. For example large machine bureaucracies are perfect for efficient mass production but not for adapting quickly to new situations. You need to consider whether the sender and receiver organisational structures are sufficiently different to warrant action. How are the top management, middle management, support and technical staff and operating core structured and interrelated? Is one firm highly compartmentalised while the other has lots of cross-

*This is an area where an external view, perhaps from a facilitator, can be valuable. A sure-fire way of spotting problems early is to bring managers and shopfloor personnel over from the recipient site to work in your facility before transferring a single soldering iron.*

functional teams? It is difficult to see what the transfer manager could do about any such mismatches, but it is unlikely that a manufacturing process designed for one type of organisational structure will run perfectly in another.

A European cross functional organisation licensed a complex manufacturing process to a traditional Korean firm. Korean conglomerates are typically very hierarchical, bureaucratic and functionally-oriented. The original process called for cross-functional management, so the Korean firm had to design a hybrid organisational structure to accommodate the licensed process without disrupting all of its other projects.

## *6. Host culture*

The cultural characteristics of labour in the target country can have a significant effect on the appropriateness of the host site. There are four, key questions that need to be considered.

**Is the manufacturing process dependent on host labour characteristics such as individualism and uncertainty avoidance?**
If your manufacturing process relies on team working (e.g. in a cell) then it will not be appropriate for a culture which puts greater emphasis on working and being rewarded individually. Many manufacturing processes require workers to take personal initiatives of a kind that Western managers consider insignificant. In some countries (China, for example) a worker will expect his or her job to be so tightly defined that no personal decision points exist.

The USA manager of a JV in Shanghai recalled his exasperation at what seemed at first like Chinese stubbornness. It transpired that the translation of the process documentation included instructions such as "perform step x, then step y" without indicating that a trolley had to be moved to a new position before starting step y. To a US worker it was 'obvious' that the trolley had to be moved - but Chinese workers were not accustomed to making that kind of inference.

**Does the manufacturing process use empowerment and have a scope that is appropriate to the recipient workforce's 'power distance'?**
Power distance is a measure of the number of levels in an organisation's hierarchy. In a country with a small power distance subordinates will refer all but the most minor decisions to their superior. They will have a very narrow scope of authority. Clearly if a manufacturing process is designed for 'empowered workers' who are expected to make decisions at the operational level it will fail entirely in a country with small power distance.

**Are the process job design, performance measurement and reward structures appropriate to host labour working practices?**
Another way of looking at the scope of authority issue is to assess how functionally rigid working practices are. In countries that maintain a strong trade tradition a worker will not be expected to work outside his or her narrow field.

When a French firm transferred its production instructions to Korea, Korean welders refused to perform the preparatory paint procedure. The transferror had to change the documentation to accommodate the strict Korean job design.

*Photographic or real examples of acceptable and unacceptable quality are a better way of guiding inspectors than written descriptions.*

**Does the process require some perception of quality, for example an aesthetic judgement or an approach to problem solving that may be culturally constrained?**
In countries where shopfloor personnel are unlikely to come into contact with high quality goods it can often be difficult to ensure consistent and objective quality targets. Also in some cultures problem solving is by random trial-and-error rather than the more logical 'experimental design' familiar in the West. This can prove extremely frustrating to Western managers trying to solve a problem during start-up who may find themselves watching a crowd of employees varying everything without any apparent 'logic'.

Cultural differences may lead you to adapt the process or job design and clarify documentation and problem-solving procedures.

## *7. Host climate*

**Is the manufacturing process appropriate for the target region's temperature range, humidity, rainfall and air quality?**
The operation of a manufacturing process and the storage of goods are influenced by environmental factors such as temperature, relative humidity, rainfall, and air quality. Many of these factors may not have been considered in the original process design if the home environment does not experience extreme conditions.

An American firm which developed manufacturing processes in California and then transferred them to Mexico to take advantage of low cost labour found that an electrical test became unreliable in Mexico's high humidity. This became so serious that they were forced to transfer the process back to the USA.

A UK electronics company found that its component placement equipment in India consistently performed worse than expected. It transpired that airborne dust was clogging the suction pumps in spite of manufacturer's assurances that the lines were adequately filtered.

## 8. Financing

**Is the manufacturing process appropriate for the expected cost of inventory, land and capital and foreign exchange requirements?**

The manufacturing process layout, choice of capital equipment and level of in-process inventory (WIP, goods-in and finished goods stock) will have been designed on the basis of the cost of land and capital at your current site. It is likely that these costs will differ significantly at the target location.

In countries where foreign exchange is not freely convertible or the currency is not stable, foreign currency factors will influence the appropriateness of a manufacturing process.

A process with a large imported content which is being used for a local market access strategy will be a heavy burden on foreign exchange. It can easily create a cash sink if the local currency is not freely convertible.

To balance foreign exchange consider localising as many components as possible, reducing inventory levels and looking for export opportunities.

## 9. Host government and legal issues

**Is the manufacturing process appropriate for the host country's legal demands, import duties and quotas, labour law, approval and license requirements, Government emission regulations and planning laws?**

This is a rather long-winded list. However it indicates the local policy considerations that must be taken into account.

Governments may impose restrictions on the trans-border or internal movement of capital, raw materials and parts as well as use of local resources. This will often be in the form of taxes or quotas.

Certain processes, equipment operation, job designs, working hours and shift patterns may not be appropriate for local labour laws. Governments may require licences or approvals for the manufacture of certain products or for locating a plant in a particular area. Conversely they may offer incentives for transferring particular technologies to their country. A manufacturing process's emissions (noise, pollutants, effluents, etc.) must also be compatible with local regulations.

To make matters worse it can be difficult to keep up to date with the latest regulations – which have a habit of changing frequently and with little notice. Foreign companies are also often subject to stricter controls than local companies.

An American firm transferring technology to Shanghai was forced to adapt its equipment to reduce noise emissions as it was immediately adjacent to a residential district.

*Contact local chambers of commerce (the American Chamber of Commerce is the most active in many countries) to keep up to date with relevant local factors. There are also agencies that specialise in keeping companies, who are planning to invest, informed.*

# Stage 3. Designing the transfer project

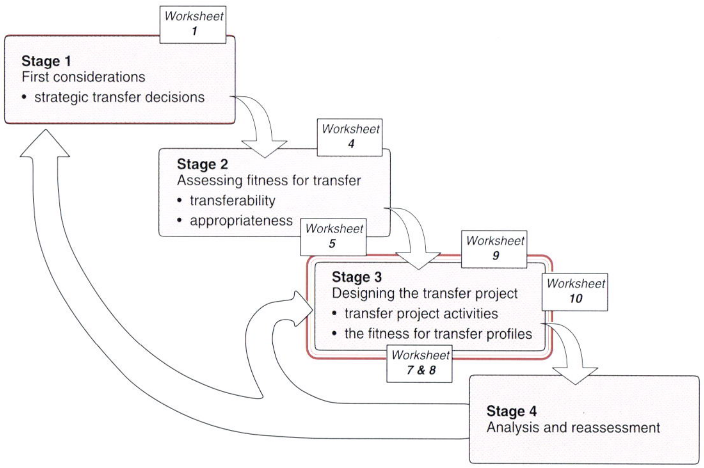


*During Stage 3 you will complete Worksheets 8 and 9 and will need to refer back to the answers you gave on Worksheets 4,5 and 7.*

## *Transfer project activities*

Now that you have considered your manufacturing process's transferability and appropriateness it is necessary to collate the transfer activities noted down along the way. You can use **Worksheet 8** to:

- list all the activities that you identified in Stage 2 when considering each of the transferability and appropriateness factors
- remove any duplicated activities
- arrange the remaining ones in order of importance and difficulty
- consider the resources that you need for each one - training requirements, support services, equipment installation engineers, suppliers, documentation, pilot activities, equipment adaptation services and software programmers

You should also look for conflict areas such as:

- the process needs changing but it is not adaptable
- the product needs modifying but this is difficult to achieve
- the host needs to develop its capabilities but the required knowledge is tacitly held

**Worksheet 7** lists the types of knowledge that you identified in your manufacturing process. You should now note down methods for transferring them (including approximate training times). Remember truly tacit knowledge can take a long time to acquire and even longer to regenerate from scratch. We have identified a number of methods for tackling the transfer of tacit knowledge:

- use on the job training/apprenticeships to transfer *truly* tacit knowledge
- capture knowledge that can be specified in a transferable form (e.g. documents, videos, cause-effect diagrams)
- redesign the process to avoid the need for truly tacit knowledge
- experiment to raise the level of knowledge and try to codify it (e.g. in hardware)
- allow for extensive support during and after the transfer in areas where tacit knowledge needs to be drawn upon (e.g. problem solving, changeovers)

Table 2 (opposite) suggests possible transfer methods for each knowledge form.

| Knowledge form | Transfer method |
|---|---|
| *Explicit* | Transfer of documents and equipment |
| *Tacit specifiable* | Externalisation:<br>• capture in documents (make explicit)<br>• rationalise behaviour<br>• metaphor and analogy<br>• common sense<br>• fishbone diagrams and other graphical representations |
| *Truly tacit* | Socialisation:<br>• on the job training<br>• apprenticeship<br><br>Regeneration at host |

*Table 2. Possible transfer methods for each form of knowledge*

**Worksheet 4**

# Measuring transferability

## Dimensions

| Key factors<br>*Properties* | Totally non-transferable | Totally transferable |
|---|---|---|
| **Knowledge** | | |
| *Amount and stage of knowledge* | Ignorance | Science |
| *Dependence on truly tacit knowledge* | High | Low |
| *Knowledge is teachable* | Not at all | Very |
| *Process has been transferred before* | Never | Often |
| **Customised and obsolete processes** | | |
| *Technology is customised, redundant or obsolete* | Very | Not at all |
| *Documentation is up-to-date and representative* | Not at all | Very |
| **Process adaptability** | | |
| *Availability of alternatives* | None | Many |
| *Need for pilot* | High | Low |
| **Packaging for transfer** | | |
| *Ability to transfer SKD or CKD* | Low | High |
| *Ability to split processes into sub-processes* | Low | High |
| *Ability to protect IPR* | Low | High |

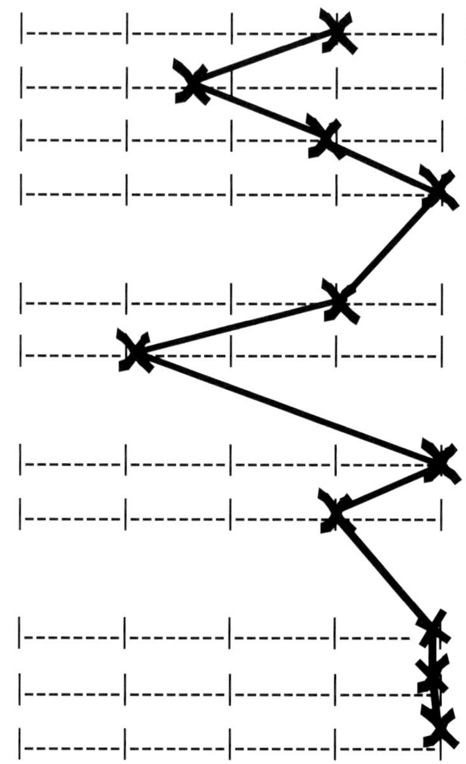

*Figure 4. Example of a completed Worksheet 4 showing a possible transferability profile*

### *The fitness for transfer profiles*

Refer to the answers you gave on **Worksheets 4 and 5** during Stage 2.

For each of the key factors of transferability and appropriateness you were asked to place an 'x' on a scale. By joining up the 'x's you will have a transferability and appropriateness profile for your manufacturing process relative to a given location (see Figure 4 opposite).

These profiles provide at-a-glance summaries of how fit for transfer your manufacturing process is. You can quickly spot where action is needed and where potential pitfalls may lie. They also provide a concise method of communicating your transfer plans to colleagues.

Use **Worksheet 9** to summarise the transferability and appropriateness of your process.

The value of this fitness for transfer assessment lies mainly in the comprehensive checklists that you filled out in Stage 2. However, it is useful to assess whether, on balance, the manufacturing process under study has high or low appropriateness and transferability. This is a subjective assessment. This exercise has real value if you are comparing a number of processes or locations.

You can now plot your manufacturing process on an A-T Matrix provided in **Worksheet 10**. This matrix links the transfer characteristics of the manufacturing process, its appropriateness (A) and transferability (T), with the activities needed to transfer it. The nearer the top right corner, the fitter for transfer.

The A-T Matrix provides a means for comparing the fitness for transfer of different manufacturing processes and for comparing different locations, partners and transfer channels.

## FAQ's

**Is there a scale for fitness for transfer?**

No. It is a subjective summary of the individual scales of the transferability and appropriateness factors (on **Worksheet 9**) which themselves are a subjective summary of the individual scales of their properties.

# Stage 4. Analysis and reassessment

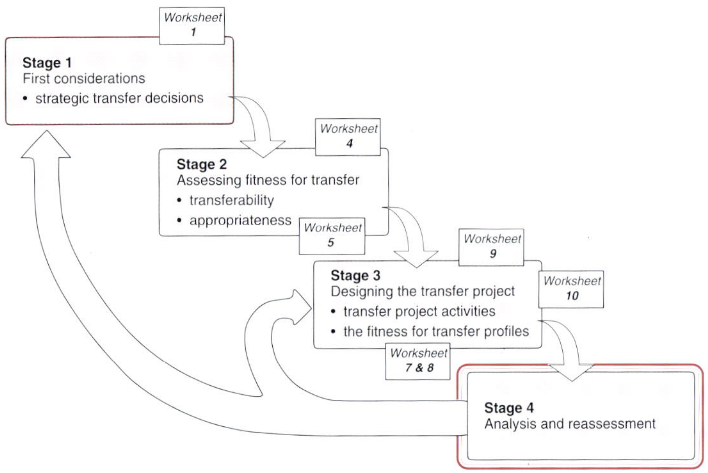


*During Stage 4 you will complete Worksheet 10 and 11 and may need to refer back to the answers you gave on Worksheets 1, 4, 5 and 9.*

*Consider splitting the manufacturing process into sub-processes. Those that are 'fit for transfer' can then be moved to the new site while the rest can stay at the current home site (or consider transferring them to a location where they are more appropriate). Plot an appropriateness and transferability profile for each sub-process and locate them on the A-T Matrix (Worksheet 10). You may even identify opportunities for transfer that you had not previously considered.*

This stage allows you to reflect on your strategic decisions and plan for transfer activities. It lets you check for consistency and identify opportunities to improve your transfer project.

Figure 5 (opposite) shows the A - T matrix that can be constructed with high and low levels of appropriateness set against high and low levels of transferability. A copy of the matrix is given on **Worksheet 10.** The actions needed to deal with the four possible circumstances are entered in each of the four quadrants of this matrix. For example, in the worst case scenario of low appropriateness and low transferability (bottom left quadrant) very high levels of activity are indicated at both home and host sites. In fact a technology transfer exercise needing so many expensive resources should probably be abandoned.

Use **Worksheet 10** to show you the appropriate quadrant on the matrix for your technology. **Worksheet 8** will tell you the actions that you need to take. If there is a large discrepancy between the actions described in the appropriate quadrant of Figure 3 and the actions described by you in **Worksheet 8**, go back and check that:

- you have positioned this transfer in the correct quadrant of the matrix
- you have taken all relevant material into account when proposing actions

| Transferability | Appropriateness: low | Appropriateness: high |
|---|---|---|
| high | *Transfer equipment and documentation.*<br><br>*Adapt process and develop host.* | *Transfer equipment and documentation.*<br><br>*Training.* |
| low | *Adapt, package, train, support, develop host (and home). Transfer equipment and documentation.* | *Transfer equipment and documentation.*<br><br>*Train and package.* |

*Figure 5. The A-T matrix showing transfer activities*

| Strategic Transfer Decision | Appropriateness | Transferability | *Fitness for transfer* |
|---|---|---|---|
| **Mode of foreign involvement** | A process that is inappropriate for a given location is more suited to export. | A process that is non-transferable is more suited to export. | A process that is unfit for transfer is more suited to export. |
| **New facility strategy** | A process's appropriateness for a given location should match the strategy for that site, e.g. ability to take advantage of low cost factors of production. | A process that is non-transferable is less suited to a strategy that requires high technical activities at the host site. | The fit for transfer parts of the process should be transferred while unfit parts are kept at the home site. Hence an international division of the process should guide the strategy. |
| **Transfer channel** | An inappropriate process, which demands the development of host characteristics requires a 'close' transfer mode. | A process that has low transferability will require a 'close' transfer mode. A process that is transferable is suitable for any mode. | Foreign Direct Investment (FDI) is a more suitable method for transferring low fitness processes. As the fitness increases, then more 'distant' modes become feasible. |
| **Location decision** | If a number of locations are available then the one for which the manufacturing process is most appropriate will be favoured. | | |
| **Partner selection** | If a number of partners are available then the one for which the manufacturing process is most appropriate will be favoured. | A partner who is more familiar with the manufacturing process will be more able to assimilate a non-transferable process. | Partner selection becomes increasingly important as process fitness decreases. |
| **Process** | If a number of technologies are available then the one that is most appropriate for a given location will be favoured. | If a number of technologies are available, then the one that is most transferable will be favoured. | Fitness provides a way of comparing the suitability for transfer of different technologies. |
| **Product** | If a number of products are available then the one whose process is most appropriate for a given location will be favoured. | If a number of products are available, then the one whose process is most transferable will be favoured. | Fitness provides a way of comparing the manufacturing processes of different products in terms of their suitability for transfer. |

*Table 3. Scenario planning using fitness for transfer*

## *Reflecting on strategic transfer decisions*

At the outset of the fitness for transfer assessment you were asked to record the strategic transfer decisions driving this transfer (**Worksheet 1**). During the assessment you may have found that the manufacturing process was inappropriate for some of the chosen location or partner characteristics. Similarly you may have found that, after such close examination, there is too much tacit knowledge to be easily transferred by a license agreement or that the planned partner has an incompatible culture or corporate structure. Now is the time to reflect on those decisions, and consider possible modifications. Table 3 (opposite) shows how appropriateness, transferability and fitness for transfer relate to each of the strategic transfer decisions.

Use **Worksheet 11** to record the different possible scenarios, barriers and opportunities posed by changing each strategic decision.

If you want to consider a different process or sub-process, location, transfer channel, partner or product then run through the appropriateness assessment in Stage 2 again. Make profiles on copies of **Worksheet 5** to compare them objectively. If you plan to compare different processes then rerun the transferability assessment and plot profiles on copies of **Worksheet 4**. Superimpose the results of each onto copies of the profiles on **Worksheet 9** and onto an A-T Matrix (**Worksheet 10**).

At the outset of this assessment we asked whether you were planning to transfer or export. This is to emphasise that export may be a more economically viable option once all of the transferability and appropriateness costs are taken into consideration. If you need to perform a cost-based scenario then Stage 3 should have provided a guideline for calculating the majority of the major transfer expenses (excluding travel and expatriate costs).

## FAQ's

**If I am planning a JV or license agreement (or even a transfer to an established subsidiary or an acquisition) what capabilities does the recipient need?**

This is a question of 'capability profiling'. Remember from the ball throwing analogy that this exercise only helps you identify the characteristics of the ball (the manufacturing process being transferred). The fitness assessment can however help you derive a capability profile - at least to some extent. For example:

- determination of the host organisation's appropriateness should point to shortfalls in the recipient's resources and capabilities
- the knowledge issues identified in the transferability assessment will suggest how receptive the recipient will need to be to new ideas and skills
- some location issues may guide the choice of partner

*In Stage 3 we showed how the different forms of knowledge require different transfer modes. Each transfer channel demonstrates a different ability to accommodate these transfer modes. For example if apprenticeships are needed to transfer tacit knowledge then this is more suited to a JV or WFOE than to a license agreement - unless provision for training is specifically made.*

# Further reading

1 Ferdows K, **'Making the Most of Foreign Factories'**, *Harvard Business Review, 1997,* March-April, pp. 73-88. A very readable article on the different reasons for transferring technology and the various types of factory that can be set up to meet these different situations.

2 Flaherty M T, **'Global Operations Management'**, *New York: McGraw-Hill, 1996*. One of the best of a recent crop of books covering the new challenges posed by operating at a global level.

3 Schmenner R W, **'Making Business Location Decisions'**, *London: Prentice Hall 1982*. This book covers comprehensively the choice of location decision.

4 Cerny, K; Bartmess, A; Wheelwright, S C and Flaherty, M T, **'Kodak Business Imaging Systems Division'**, *HBS Case 693-043, Boston: HBS Press 1992*. Although difficult to obtain (try the Harvard Business School website at http://www.hbs.edu), the case of Kodak's relocation decision includes a great deal of useful analysis.

# FITNESS FOR TRANSFER WORKPACK

## Worksheet 1. Strategic transfer decisions

| | *Tick one from each section* ✓ |
|---|---|
| 1. Mode of involvement<br>Export | |
| Manufacture overseas | |
| 2. New facility strategy<br>Source | |
| Off-shore | |
| Lead | |
| Outpost | |
| Contributor | |
| Server | |
| 3. Transfer channel<br>Wholly foreign-owned enterprise | |
| Acquisition | |
| Joint venture | |
| License agreement | |
| Equipment sale | |

| | *Details* |
|---|---|
| 4. Location | |
| 5. Partner | |
| 6. Process | |
| 7. Product | |

## Worksheet 2. Manufacturing process issues

Product name:

Date:

Completed by:

| Question | Yes | No | Both/Equal | Don't Know |
|---|---|---|---|---|
| Is the competitiveness of the process primarily determined by the knowledge and skills of the people who process it (rather than the technology itself)? | ☐ | ☐ | ☐ | ☐ |
| Is your process labour rather than capital intensive? | ☐ | ☐ | ☐ | ☐ |
| Is the manufacturing process **un**affected by changes in climate? | ☐ | ☐ | | ☐ |
| Is the quality of supplied material critical? | ☐ | ☐ | | ☐ |
| Can the manufacturing process be designed to have different economies of scale? | ☐ | ☐ | | ☐ |
| Is the manufacturing process highly dependent on certain critical resources and capabilities? (e.g. cranes, marketing, steam power) | ☐ | ☐ | | ☐ |
| Can the manufacturing process be split into sub-processes? | ☐ | ☐ | | ☐ |
| Does the process use Just in Time (JIT) delivery? | ☐ | ☐ | | ☐ |

## Worksheet 3. Transfer issues

Product name:

Date:

Completed by:

| Question | Yes | No | Both/Equal | Don't Know |
|---|---|---|---|---|
| Will the project primarily involve training and personnel transfer (rather than the transfer of equipment and documents)? | ☐ | ☐ | ☐ | ☐ |
| Is the target country a source of low cost labour (rather than capital)? | ☐ | ☐ | ☐ | ☐ |
| Is the target country much hotter, colder or more humid than the current site? | ☐ | ☐ | | ☐ |
| Are the suppliers in the host country of equal capability to your current suppliers? | ☐ | ☐ | | ☐ |
| Will the target market require the manufacture of different volume/lot sizes to the current market? | ☐ | ☐ | | ☐ |
| Are the resources and capabilities of the recipient well-understood? (e.g. marketing, physical infrastructure) | ☐ | ☐ | | ☐ |
| Does part of the manufacturing process contain some expertise that you don't want to transfer? | ☐ | ☐ | | ☐ |
| Is the transport infrastructure in the target country good? | ☐ | ☐ | | ☐ |

## Worksheet 4. Measuring transferability

| **Key factors** *Properties* | Dimensions | | | | | |
|---|---|---|---|---|---|---|
| | **Totally Non-Transferable** | | | | | **Totally Transferable** |
| **Knowledge issues** | | | | | | |
| *Amount and stage of knowledge* | Ignorance | \|------ | \|------ | \|------ | \|------\| | Science |
| *Dependence on truly tacit knowledge* | High | \|------ | \|------ | \|------ | \|------\| | Low |
| *Knowledge is teachable* | Not at all | \|------ | \|------ | \|------ | \|------\| | Very |
| *Process has been transferred before* | Never | \|------ | \|------ | \|------ | \|------\| | Often |
| **Customised and obsolete processes** | | | | | | |
| *Technology is customised, redundant or obsolete* | Very | \|------ | \|------ | \|------ | \|------\| | Not at all |
| *Documentation is up-to-date and representative* | Not at all | \|------ | \|------ | \|------ | \|------\| | Very |
| **Process adaptability** | | | | | | |
| *Availability of alternatives* | None | \|------ | \|------ | \|------ | \|------\| | Many |
| *Need for pilot* | High | \|------ | \|------ | \|------ | \|------\| | Low |
| **Packaging for transfer** | | | | | | |
| *Ability to transfer SKD or CKD* | Low | \|------ | \|------ | \|------ | \|------\| | High |
| *Ability to split process into sub-processes* | Low | \|------ | \|------ | \|------ | \|------\| | High |
| *Ability to protect IPR* | Low | \|------ | \|------ | \|------ | \|------\| | High |

**Process:**

## Knowledge issues

**Process:**

Customised and obsolete processes

**Process:**

Process adaptability

**Process:**

Packaging for transfer

## Worksheet 5. Measuring appropriateness

Dimensions

| **Key factors** / *Properties* | **Totally inappropriate** | | | **Totally appropriate** |
|---|---|---|---|---|
| **Host labour** | | | | |
| *Productivity and cost of direct/indirect labour* | | | | |
| *Skills available from local labour pool* | | | | |
| *Education and language characteristics* | | | | |
| *Labour turnover* | | | | |
| **Target market** | | | | |
| *Process capacity and flexibility match with target market demand characteristics* | | | | |
| *Product match with target market needs* | | | | |
| **Suppliers** | | | | |
| *Quality, cost, delivery, flexibility and service of local or international suppliers* | | | | |
| **Host infrastructure** | | | | |
| *Quality, cost and availability of local utilities* | | | | |
| *Availability, cost and reliability of telecommunications and transport infrastructure* | | | | |
| *Space and format of buildings* | | | | |
| **Host organisation's resources and capabilities** | | | | |
| *Technical resources* | | | | |
| *Familiarity with manufacturing methods* | | | | |
| *Support capabilities* | | | | |
| *Organisational structure* | | | | |
| **Host culture** | | | | |
| *Degree of individualism and uncertainty avoidance* | | | | |
| *Power distance orientation* | | | | |
| *Working practices* | | | | |
| *Approach to problem solving and quality perception* | | | | |
| **Host climate** | | | | |
| *Local temperature range, humidity and air quality* | | | | |
| **Financing** | | | | |
| *Cost of inventory, cost of land and capital and foreign exchange requirement* | | | | |
| **Host government and legal issues** | | | | |
| *Legal demands, import duties and quotas, labour laws, approval and licence requirements* | | | | |
| *Government emission regulations and planning laws* | | | | |

**Process:**

Host labour

**Process:**

Target market

**Process:**

Suppliers

**Process:**

Host infrastructure

**Process:**

Host organisation's resources and capabilities

 

**Process:**

Host culture

**Process:**

Host climate

**Process:**

Financing

**Process:**

Host Government and legal issues

## Worksheet 6. "Things to find out"

*Use this sheet to identify data to be collected. This includes specific capabilities of the recipient, country characteristics and areas of critical tacit knowledge in the process.*

## Worksheet 7. Knowledge form and transfer method

| Knowledge form | Transfer method | Resource | Time |
|---|---|---|---|
| *Explicit* | | | |
| *Tacit specifiable* | | | |
| *Truly tacit* | | | |

## Worksheet 8. Transfer implementation activities

Activity

*Manufacturing process adaptation*

*Manufacturing process packaging*

*Sender and receiver development*

*Support*

## Worksheet 9. Fitness for transfer summary

Product/process name:

Location:

Partner:

Transfer type:

### Dimensions

| *Key factors* | **Inappropriate** – – – – – – – – – – **Appropriate** |
|---|---|
| **Appropriateness** | |
| *Host labour* | \|– – – – –\|– – – – –\|– – – – –\|– – – – –\| |
| *Target market* | \|– – – – –\|– – – – –\|– – – – –\|– – – – –\| |
| *Suppliers* | \|– – – – –\|– – – – –\|– – – – –\|– – – – –\| |
| *Host infrastructure* | \|– – – – –\|– – – – –\|– – – – –\|– – – – –\| |
| *Host organisation's resources and capabilities* | \|– – – – –\|– – – – –\|– – – – –\|– – – – –\| |
| *Host culture* | \|– – – – –\|– – – – –\|– – – – –\|– – – – –\| |
| *Host climate* | \|– – – – –\|– – – – –\|– – – – –\|– – – – –\| |
| *Financing* | \|– – – – –\|– – – – –\|– – – – –\|– – – – –\| |
| *Host Government and legal issues* | \|– – – – –\|– – – – –\|– – – – –\|– – – – –\| |
| **Transferability** | |
| *Knowledge issues* | \|– – – – –\|– – – – –\|– – – – –\|– – – – –\| |
| *Customised and obsolete processes* | \|– – – – –\|– – – – –\|– – – – –\|– – – – –\| |
| *Process adaptability* | \|– – – – –\|– – – – –\|– – – – –\|– – – – –\| |
| *Packaging for transfer* | \|– – – – –\|– – – – –\|– – – – –\|– – – – –\| |

*Notes:*

## Worksheet 9. Fitness for transfer summary *continued*

*Notes: continued*

## Worksheet 10. The A-T Matrix

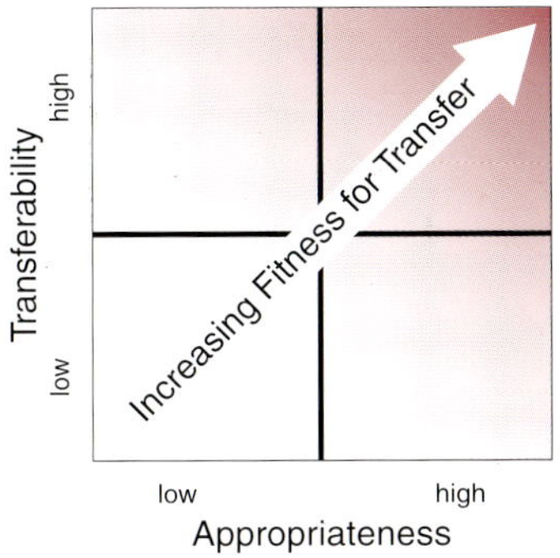


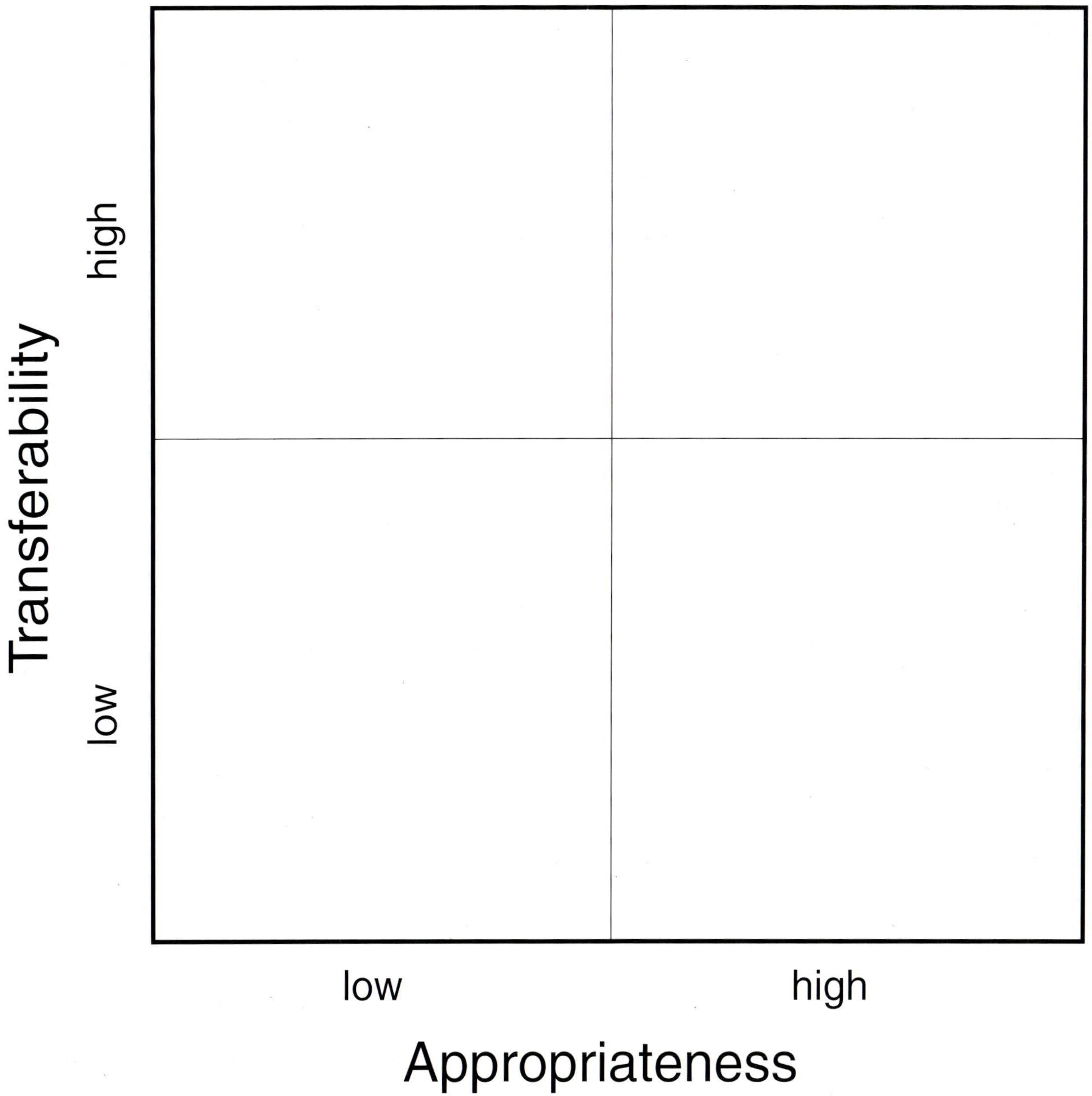

## Worksheet 10 *continued*

*Main factor affecting transferability is .....*

*Main factor affecting appropriateness is .....*

## Worksheet 11. Scenario planning

*Use this worksheet to record different transfer scenarios.*

*Variables include:*

* *Export instead of manufacture overseas*
* *Different strategy at new facility*
* *Different transfer channel*
* *Different location*
* *Different partner*
* *Different process*
* *Different product*